Pi Power

A Beginner's User Guide to Raspberry Pi 5

Jason Hills

Table Of Contents

Technical Specifications
Glossary

CHAPTER ONE : Overview of Raspberry Pi 5

The Raspberry Pi 5, the latest iteration in the popular series of single-board computers, stands at the forefront of innovation, bringing a myriad of enhancements that cater to a diverse range of users. As a compact yet powerful computing device, the Raspberry Pi 5 boasts upgraded hardware components, marking a significant evolution from its predecessors.

One of the key highlights is the enhanced processing power, featuring a more robust CPU and GPU configuration. This results in improved performance, making the Raspberry Pi 5 an ideal choice for applications ranging from basic computing tasks to more resource-intensive projects like multimedia streaming and gaming.

The GPIO (General Purpose Input/Output) pins, a hallmark of Raspberry Pi's versatility, have been expanded in the fifth iteration, providing users with increased possibilities for hardware interfacing and project development. This makes it an even more attractive platform for makers, educators, and hobbyists who seek to delve into the world of electronics and programming.

Connectivity options have also been bolstered in the Raspberry Pi 5, addressing the demands of modern applications. With upgraded Wi-Fi capabilities, faster Ethernet, and additional USB ports, users can seamlessly integrate the device into various networks and connect a broader array of peripherals.

Furthermore, improvements in graphics capabilities open up new possibilities for visual applications and projects. Whether it's image processing, video streaming, or creating graphical user interfaces, the Raspberry Pi 5's graphics enhancements offer a more immersive and responsive experience.

In essence, the Raspberry Pi 5 is a testament to the ongoing commitment of the Raspberry Pi Foundation to provide an accessible yet powerful computing platform. Its combination of enhanced hardware features positions it as a versatile tool for a wide spectrum of users, from beginners looking to explore the world of computing to seasoned developers and engineers pushing the boundaries of what can be achieved with a single-board computer.

Purpose of the User Guide

The purpose of this user guide is to serve as a comprehensive resource, offering guidance and insights to users navigating the capabilities of the Raspberry Pi 5. As an intricate device with diverse applications, the guide aims to bridge the gap between the user's curiosity and the potential of the Raspberry Pi 5.

For beginners, this guide provides a gentle introduction, demystifying the initial setup process and guiding users through the essential steps to get started. From unboxing to the first boot-up, users will find clear instructions, accompanied by visuals, ensuring a smooth and frustration-free initiation into the world of Raspberry Pi computing.

Intermediate users, already familiar with the basics, will discover in-depth explorations of the Raspberry Pi 5's features and capabilities. This includes a detailed understanding of the GPIO pins, advanced networking configurations, programming environments, and project ideas to unleash creativity. The guide aims to empower users to go beyond the standard applications and harness the full potential of the Raspberry

Pi 5 for personalized projects and endeavors.

In addition to practical instructions, the guide serves as a reference, offering troubleshooting tips and solutions for common challenges users may encounter. Whether it's resolving hardware issues, troubleshooting software errors, or optimizing performance, this user guide aims to be a companion throughout the user's Raspberry Pi 5 journey.

Ultimately, the overarching purpose is to facilitate a seamless and enjoyable experience with the Raspberry Pi 5. Whether the user is a student, hobbyist, educator, or professional, this guide strives to be an invaluable resource, unlocking the possibilities that this small yet mighty single-board computer brings to the table.

CHAPTER TWO: Getting Started

Unboxing and Setup

The journey into the Raspberry Pi 5 experience begins with the excitement of unboxing. As the user opens the package, they are greeted by a compact yet powerful computing device and an array of essential components. The first step involves understanding each component, from the Raspberry Pi board itself to the power supply, microSD card, and any included accessories.

Clear, concise instructions, complemented by visual aids, guide users through the unboxing process. The importance of handling components with care, especially the delicate nature of the microSD card and the GPIO pins, is emphasized. This section aims to instill confidence in users, ensuring they are ready for the subsequent steps in their Raspberry Pi journey.

Moving on to the setup, users are guided through assembling the hardware components. This includes attaching the power supply, connecting peripherals such as keyboards and mice, and establishing a link to an external display. The user is provided with insights into choosing the right peripherals, ensuring compatibility, and addressing common pitfalls encountered during the setup process.

Connecting Peripherals

With the hardware components assembled, the next crucial step is connecting peripherals. This encompasses a variety of devices, including input devices like keyboards and mice, output devices like displays, and additional accessories such as cameras or sensors. Each peripheral has its place in the Raspberry Pi ecosystem, contributing to the device's versatility.

Detailed instructions are provided for USB and HDMI connections, ensuring users understand the significance of each port. For users keen on wireless connectivity, guidance on connecting Bluetooth devices and configuring Wi-Fi settings is included. The guide also addresses the utilization of USB hubs for expanding the range of connected devices, a valuable tip for those with ambitious projects requiring multiple peripherals.

Special attention is given to the GPIO pins, showcasing their role in interfacing with external hardware. Users are introduced to the concept of breadboarding and encouraged to explore the world of physical computing by connecting LEDs, sensors, and other electronic components to these pins. This hands-on approach fosters a deeper understanding of the Raspberry Pi's capabilities and opens the door to limitless project possibilities.

Powering On and Initial Configuration

The culmination of unboxing and connecting peripherals leads to the pivotal moment of powering on the Raspberry Pi 5. Users are guided through the power-up sequence, ensuring that the power supply is stable, the microSD card is securely inserted, and all connections are intact. Common issues related to power, such as inadequate power supply or loose connections, are addressed to prevent frustration at this crucial stage.

As the Raspberry Pi 5 boots up, users are introduced to the initial configuration process. This involves selecting language preferences, setting up Wi-Fi connectivity, and creating user accounts. Clear, step-by-step instructions demystify these essential configuration steps, ensuring users of all technical levels can navigate the process with ease.

The guide delves into the Raspbian operating system, providing an overview of its interface and functionalities. Users are introduced to the desktop environment and the terminal, laying the foundation for both graphical and command-line interactions. This section aims to make users feel comfortable in their new digital environment, setting the stage for further exploration and learning.

Emphasis is placed on updating the system to ensure it is equipped with the latest software and security patches. This proactive approach promotes a stable and secure computing environment for users. Additionally, guidance is provided on installing essential software packages, empowering users to customize their Raspberry Pi 5 according to their specific needs and interests.

In essence, the "Getting Started" section is a comprehensive initiation into the Raspberry Pi 5 experience. From the thrill of unboxing to the practicalities of connecting peripherals and the intricacies of powering on and configuring the device, users are equipped with the knowledge and confidence needed for their Raspberry Pi journey. This foundational understanding paves the way for deeper exploration into the capabilities of the Raspberry Pi 5 in subsequent sections of the user guide.

CHAPTER THREE: Understanding Raspberry Pi 5

Hardware Components

A detailed understanding of the hardware components is essential for maximizing the potential of the Raspberry Pi 5. At its core, the Raspberry Pi 5 features a powerful system-on-chip (SoC) incorporating a robust CPU and GPU configuration. This enhanced processing power, compared to previous models, empowers users to engage in a broader range of applications, from basic computing tasks to more resource-intensive projects like multimedia streaming and image processing.

Accompanying the CPU and GPU are generous memory options, facilitating smooth multitasking and efficient handling of data. Users benefit from ample RAM, providing a responsive computing experience. The presence of USB ports,

HDMI outputs, and a microSD card slot enhances the device's connectivity, enabling users to connect a variety of peripherals and expand storage capacity.

Networking components play a pivotal role in the Raspberry Pi 5's functionality. Ethernet ports provide reliable wired connectivity, while upgraded Wi-Fi capabilities ensure seamless wireless networking. These components collectively form the foundation of the Raspberry Pi 5's capabilities, creating a versatile platform for diverse applications.

GPIO Pins and Expansion Options

The GPIO (General Purpose Input/Output) pins are a hallmark of Raspberry Pi's versatility, enabling users to interact with the physical world through electronic components. In the Raspberry Pi 5, the GPIO pins have been expanded, offering users even more opportunities for hardware interfacing and project development.

Users are introduced to the GPIO layout, understanding the functions of each pin and their relevance to specific tasks. Practical examples illustrate how GPIO pins can be utilized to connect LEDs, sensors, motors, and other electronic components. This hands-on exploration fosters a deeper understanding of physical computing and encourages users to embark on creative projects.

Expansion options extend beyond the GPIO pins, encompassing various add-ons and HATs (Hardware Attached on Top). Users are guided through the process of connecting and configuring these additional hardware components. Whether it's a camera module for capturing images and video, a sensor array for environmental monitoring, or a motor controller for robotics projects, the Raspberry Pi 5's expansion options cater to a wide array of interests and applications.

The guide also delves into the software aspect of GPIO interaction, introducing users to programming languages such as Python for controlling electronic components. Code snippets and examples provide a practical foundation for users keen on exploring the intersection of software and hardware.

Networking Features

Networking is a crucial aspect of the Raspberry Pi 5, enabling users to connect the device to local networks and the internet. The Ethernet port provides a stable wired connection, suitable for scenarios where reliability is paramount. Users are guided through the process of connecting via Ethernet, configuring network settings, and troubleshooting common connectivity issues.

Wireless networking is another key feature, with upgraded Wi-Fi capabilities ensuring faster and more reliable wireless connections. The guide provides step-by-step instructions for configuring Wi-Fi settings, connecting to different networks, and troubleshooting wireless connectivity problems.

Remote access is a prominent feature enabled by networking. Users are introduced to SSH (Secure Shell), a protocol that allows for secure command-line access to the Raspberry Pi 5 over a network. This feature is particularly useful for headless setups, where the Raspberry Pi is operated without a connected monitor, keyboard, or mouse.

The guide also explores more advanced networking concepts, such as setting up the Raspberry Pi as a network-attached storage (NAS) device, configuring a VPN (Virtual

Private Network), and utilizing the device as a web server. These capabilities showcase the Raspberry Pi 5's potential for diverse networking applications, making it a valuable tool for both home and professional use.

In summary, the "Understanding Raspberry Pi 5" section serves as a comprehensive exploration of the device's hardware and networking features. From the core components that drive its performance to the GPIO pins that enable physical computing, and the networking capabilities that connect it to the wider digital landscape, users gain a holistic understanding of the Raspberry Pi 5's capabilities. This knowledge lays the groundwork for further exploration and project development in subsequent sections of the user guide.

CHAPTER FOUR: Operating System Installation

Choosing an OS

Selecting the right operating system (OS) is a pivotal decision in the journey of unleashing the full potential of the Raspberry Pi 5. The Raspberry Pi ecosystem offers a variety of OS options, each tailored to different needs and preferences. Understanding the characteristics of these operating systems is crucial for users to align their Raspberry Pi with their specific goals.

Raspbian (now Raspberry Pi OS):

As the official OS developed by the Raspberry Pi Foundation, Raspberry Pi OS (formerly known as Raspbian) is a natural choice for many users. Tailored specifically for Raspberry Pi hardware, it provides a user-friendly interface and a range of pre-installed software. Its stability and compatibility make it an excellent starting point for beginners and those exploring educational applications.

Ubuntu for Raspberry Pi:

For users familiar with Ubuntu on desktop or server environments, there's an official version optimized for the Raspberry Pi. This brings the familiarity and robustness of Ubuntu to the Raspberry Pi platform, making it an attractive choice for users who want a consistent experience across devices.

Arch Linux ARM:

For those seeking a more hands-on and customizable experience, Arch Linux ARM provides a lightweight and flexible OS. Its rolling release model ensures users have access to the latest software packages, and its minimalistic approach allows for a more tailored and efficient system setup.

Other Specialized OS Options:

Beyond the well-known options, there are specialized operating systems designed for specific purposes. For example, if users are interested in turning their Raspberry Pi into a media center, they might opt for LibreELEC or OSMC. If IoT (Internet of Things) projects are the focus, Raspbian Lite or Ubuntu Server might be more suitable.

Guidance in the user guide assists users in making an informed decision based on their intended use, level of experience, and personal preferences. Key considerations include the availability of software packages, community support, and the balance between user-friendly interfaces and customization options.

Installation Steps

Once users have chosen the operating system that aligns with their goals, the next step is navigating the installation process. This section of the user guide provides a step-by-step walkthrough, demystifying the installation procedure and ensuring users of all technical backgrounds can successfully set up their chosen OS.

1. Downloading the OS Image:

Users are guided to the official website of their chosen OS, where they can download the disk image. Clear instructions highlight the importance of choosing the correct version that is compatible with the Raspberry Pi 5.

2. Preparing the MicroSD Card:

The microSD card is the storage medium for the Raspberry Pi OS. Detailed steps are provided for formatting the microSD card, ensuring it is ready to receive the OS image. Users are also informed about the minimum recommended size for the microSD card to accommodate the OS and potential future software installations.

3. Flashing the OS Image:

The guide walks users through the process of flashing the downloaded OS image onto the microSD card. Various tools, such as Etcher or Raspberry Pi Imager, are recommended for this task. Users are informed about the importance of safely ejecting the microSD card to prevent data corruption.

4. Initial Configuration:

After the OS image is successfully flashed onto the microSD card, users proceed to insert the card into the Raspberry Pi 5. The guide covers the initial boot-up process, ensuring users are prepared to navigate the first-time setup wizard.

5. Setting up Wi-Fi and User Accounts:

As part of the initial configuration, users are prompted to set up Wi-Fi connectivity and create user accounts. Clear instructions guide users through these essential steps, ensuring a seamless transition into the operating system.

6. Updating and Upgrading:

Following the installation, users are encouraged to perform system updates and upgrades. This ensures that the Raspberry Pi OS is equipped with the latest security patches and software enhancements. Users are provided with commands for updating the system through the terminal.

7. Exploring the Desktop Environment:

As users successfully boot into the operating system, they are introduced to the desktop environment. Navigation tips, an overview of pre-installed software, and guidance on accessing the terminal set the stage for further exploration.

This comprehensive guide to operating system installation serves as a vital resource for users at every stage of their Raspberry Pi journey. From selecting the right OS for their needs to navigating the intricacies of installation, users gain the knowledge and confidence needed to harness the full capabilities of their Raspberry Pi 5. The user guide sets the foundation for further exploration in subsequent sections, where users can dive into programming, project development, and advanced customization.

CHAPTER FIVE: Basic Usage

Navigating the Desktop Environment

The desktop environment is the graphical user interface (GUI) that provides users with a visual way to interact with the Raspberry Pi 5. Navigating this environment is essential for users who prefer a point-and-click approach to accessing applications, files, and settings.

1. Desktop Layout:

Users are introduced to the elements of the desktop, including the taskbar, menu bar, and desktop icons. Clear explanations guide users through the purpose and functionality of each component.

2. Menu Navigation:

The menu bar, typically located at the top of the screen, is explored in detail. Users learn how to access applications, settings, and system tools through the menu. Special attention is given to the Raspberry Pi menu, where users can find essential tools and preferences.

3. Application Launching:

Step-by-step instructions are provided for launching applications from the desktop or menu. Users gain insights into organizing and customizing the desktop for quick access to frequently used programs.

4. Virtual Desktops and Workspaces:

The concept of virtual desktops and workspaces is introduced, allowing users to organize their tasks and applications efficiently. Users learn how to switch between different desktops and utilize this feature for improved multitasking.

5. Customization:

Users are encouraged to personalize their desktop environment. The guide covers aspects such as changing wallpapers, adjusting themes, and configuring desktop preferences to create a workspace that suits individual preferences.

Using Terminal Commands

While the desktop environment provides a user-friendly interface, mastering the use of terminal commands opens a gateway to a deeper level of control and customization. This section of the user guide empowers users to harness the power of the command line for efficient and precise interactions with the Raspberry Pi 5.

1. Accessing the Terminal:

Clear instructions guide users on how to access the terminal. Whether it's through the desktop menu or keyboard shortcuts, users become familiar with opening the command-line interface.

2. Basic Commands:

Essential terminal commands are introduced, starting with navigation commands (cd, ls) and file manipulation commands (cp, mv, rm). Users gain confidence in navigating directories, listing files, and managing their file system through the command line.

3. Text Editing:

Users are introduced to basic text editors like Nano or Vim, enabling them to create and edit text files directly from the terminal.

This skill is fundamental for scripting, programming, and configuration tasks.

4. Package Management:

The guide covers package management commands (apt-get or apt) for installing, updating, and removing software packages. Users understand the importance of keeping their system up-to-date and managing software installations efficiently.

5. User Permissions:

Understanding user permissions is essential for maintaining a secure and well-organized system. The guide explores commands related to user permissions, such as chmod and chown, empowering users to control access to files and directories.

6. System Information:

Users learn commands for retrieving system information, including hardware details, resource utilization, and network information. This knowledge is valuable for troubleshooting and monitoring the Raspberry Pi's performance.

7. Scripting and Automation:

As users become comfortable with terminal commands, the guide introduces the concept of scripting. Basic scripting languages like Bash are explored, enabling users to automate repetitive tasks and customize their Raspberry Pi environment.

File Management

Efficient file management is at the core of a well-organized and functional computing experience. This section of the user guide equips users with the skills to navigate, organize, and manipulate files and directories effectively.

1. Navigating Directories:

Building on the basic navigation commands introduced earlier, users explore how to move between directories, understand directory structures, and access files in different locations.

2. Creating and Deleting Files:

Clear instructions guide users on how to create new files and delete existing ones. Whether it's through the desktop environment or terminal commands, users gain confidence in managing their file system.

3. Copying and Moving Files:

Users learn techniques for copying files to different locations and moving them between directories. These skills are fundamental for organizing files and distributing data across the Raspberry Pi's storage.

4. Archiving and Compression:

The guide covers commands for creating archives (tar) and compressing files (gzip), allowing users to efficiently manage large sets of data and backup important files.

5. Searching for Files:

Efficient file searching techniques are introduced, both through the graphical file manager and the command line. Users discover how to locate specific files or directories within the system.

6. File Permissions and Ownership:

Building on the concepts introduced in the terminal commands section, users delve deeper into managing file permissions and ownership. This knowledge is crucial for maintaining security and controlling access to sensitive data.

7. Graphical File Managers:

Users are introduced to graphical file managers available in the desktop environment, providing an alternative to command-line file management. This section offers guidance on using file managers effectively for tasks such as moving, copying, and deleting files.

In conclusion, the "Basic Usage" section of the user guide serves as a comprehensive resource for users to navigate the graphical desktop environment, utilize terminal commands effectively, and master the art of file management. Whether users prefer a point-and-click approach or seek the efficiency of the command line, this section provides the foundation for a confident and efficient Raspberry Pi 5 experience.

CHAPTER SIX: Programming on Raspberry Pi 5

Introduction to Python (and other programming languages)

Programming on the Raspberry Pi 5 opens up a world of possibilities, from creating simple scripts to developing complex applications and projects. This section of the user guide serves as a gentle introduction, providing users with the foundation to start their programming journey, focusing particularly on Python, a versatile and beginner-friendly language widely supported on the Raspberry Pi.

1. Understanding Python:

Users are introduced to Python, highlighting its readability, simplicity, and versatility. Python's syntax is explained in a beginner-friendly manner, emphasizing its role as an excellent language for both beginners and experienced developers.

2. Setting Up Python:

Step-by-step instructions guide users in setting up Python on their Raspberry Pi 5. Whether Python is pre-installed or needs to be installed manually, users gain confidence in preparing their environment for programming.

3. Interactive Mode and Scripting:

The guide introduces Python's interactive mode, allowing users to experiment with code snippets directly in the terminal. Users also learn the basics of scripting, creating and executing Python scripts to perform specific tasks.

4. Basic Python Concepts:

Core programming concepts, such as variables, data types, conditionals, loops, and functions, are explained in a beginner-friendly manner. Practical examples illustrate how these concepts are applied in Python programming.

5. Working with Data:

Users are guided through manipulating data structures in Python, including lists, dictionaries, and tuples. Practical exercises demonstrate how to store, retrieve, and modify data, laying the foundation for more advanced programming tasks.

6. Introduction to Libraries and Modules:

Python's strength lies in its extensive standard library and third-party modules. Users are introduced to the concept of libraries and modules, exploring how to leverage pre-built functionalities to enhance their projects without reinventing the wheel.

7. Project-Based Learning:

Emphasis is placed on project-based learning to reinforce programming concepts. Users are encouraged to embark on small projects, such as creating a simple calculator, automating tasks, or developing text-based games, to apply their newfound Python skills.

Beyond Python, the user guide acknowledges the diverse programming landscape and provides brief introductions to other languages suitable for Raspberry Pi development. These may include JavaScript for web-based projects, C/C++ for performance-critical applications, or Java for cross-platform development.

Development Tools and IDEs

Selecting the right development tools and integrated development environments (IDEs) significantly enhances the programming experience on the Raspberry Pi 5. This section of the user guide explores various tools and IDEs, helping users find the environment that best suits their preferences and project requirements.

1. IDLE - Python's Default IDE:

   As the default IDE for Python on Raspberry Pi, IDLE is introduced. Users learn how to navigate the IDLE environment, write, run, and debug Python code. Its simplicity makes it an ideal starting point for beginners.

2. **Thonny IDE:

Thonny, a beginner-friendly Python IDE, is explored in detail. Users are guided through its features, including a built-in package manager, code execution, and debugging capabilities. Thonny's user-friendly interface makes it an excellent choice for those starting with Python programming.

3. Visual Studio Code (VSCode):

More advanced users looking for a versatile and feature-rich IDE may opt for Visual Studio Code. The guide provides instructions for installing and configuring VSCode on the Raspberry Pi 5, highlighting its powerful extensions, integrated terminal, and debugging capabilities.

4. **Geany:

Geany, a lightweight and fast IDE, is introduced as an alternative for users who prefer simplicity without sacrificing essential features. The guide covers its installation and basic usage, making it accessible for users with varying levels of programming experience.

5. Command-Line Tools:

Acknowledging that some users may prefer a more minimalistic approach, the guide introduces command-line tools for programming on the Raspberry Pi. Users learn how to use a text editor (e.g., Nano or Vim) and the terminal for writing and executing code without a graphical interface.

6. Remote Development:

As an advanced topic, the guide briefly explores remote development options. Users discover how to use VSCode's remote development extension or SSH to connect to their Raspberry Pi 5 and perform coding tasks from their primary development machine.

7. Version Control with Git:

Users are introduced to version control using Git, an essential skill for collaborative and organized programming. The guide covers basic Git commands, initializing repositories, and pushing code to platforms like GitHub for collaborative development.

In conclusion, the "Programming on Raspberry Pi 5" section of the user guide provides a comprehensive introduction to programming, focusing on Python as the primary language. Users gain a solid foundation in Python programming concepts and are equipped with the knowledge to choose the right development tools and IDEs for their projects. Whether users are beginners exploring the world of coding or experienced developers diving into Raspberry Pi development, this section serves as a valuable resource for programming success.

CHAPTER SEVEN: Networking and Connectivity

Configuring Wi-Fi and Ethernet

Networking is a fundamental aspect of the Raspberry Pi 5's functionality, allowing users to connect the device to local networks and the internet. This section of the user guide delves into the intricacies of configuring Wi-Fi and Ethernet, providing step-by-step instructions for users to establish stable and reliable connections.

1. Wi-Fi Configuration:

Users are guided through the process of configuring Wi-Fi on their Raspberry Pi 5. Clear instructions cover accessing the desktop environment's network settings or utilizing terminal commands for headless setups. Important considerations, such as security protocols (WPA2, WPA3), SSID, and password entry, are emphasized to ensure a secure and seamless connection.

2. Ethernet Configuration:

For users opting for a wired connection, Ethernet configuration is explored. The guide covers connecting the Raspberry Pi 5 to a router or switch using an Ethernet cable. Users learn how to configure static or dynamic IP addresses, understanding the implications of each choice in different network scenarios.

3. Network Troubleshooting:

Troubleshooting tips are provided for common network issues. Users learn how to diagnose problems related to Wi-Fi or Ethernet connectivity, such as incorrect credentials, IP address conflicts, or hardware issues. This troubleshooting knowledge ensures users can address connectivity challenges effectively.

4. Advanced Network Settings:

Advanced users are introduced to additional network settings, such as configuring a static IP address for more control over network configurations. This knowledge is valuable for users with specific networking requirements or those setting up dedicated servers on their Raspberry Pi 5.

5. Switching Between Networks:

Users who frequently move their Raspberry Pi 5 between different Wi-Fi networks learn how to seamlessly switch between networks without encountering connectivity issues. This skill is particularly useful for users with mobile or portable Raspberry Pi projects.

Remote Access and SSH

Remote access is a powerful feature that allows users to control and manage their Raspberry Pi 5 from another device, enhancing flexibility and convenience. This section of the user guide focuses on SSH (Secure Shell), a secure protocol for establishing remote connections to the Raspberry Pi 5.

1. Enabling SSH:

Users are guided through the process of enabling SSH on their Raspberry Pi 5. This involves accessing the Raspberry Pi Configuration tool in the desktop environment or creating an empty file named "ssh" on the boot partition for headless setups. Ensuring SSH is enabled is the first step in establishing remote access.

2. SSH Client Configuration:

Users learn how to use SSH clients on their primary machines to connect to the Raspberry Pi 5. Clear instructions cover the syntax for connecting via the terminal, specifying the Raspberry Pi's IP address or hostname, and using the default username and password.

3. SSH Key Authentication:

For enhanced security, users are introduced to SSH key authentication. The guide covers generating SSH key pairs, configuring the Raspberry Pi 5 to accept key-based authentication, and connecting without entering a password. This method ensures a more secure and streamlined remote access experience.

4. Remote Desktop Access:

Beyond command-line access, users exploring graphical interfaces remotely discover how to set up remote desktop access. The guide introduces tools like VNC (Virtual Network Computing) for users who prefer a graphical user interface when remotely controlling their Raspberry Pi 5.

5. Securing Remote Access:

Best practices for securing remote access are highlighted. Users learn how to change default usernames and passwords, disable password authentication in favor of SSH keys, and implement firewall rules to restrict access. These measures enhance the security of remote connections and protect the Raspberry Pi 5 from unauthorized access.

6.SSH Port Forwarding:

Advanced users are introduced to SSH port forwarding, a technique that enables secure access to services running on the Raspberry Pi 5. This knowledge is valuable for users hosting web servers, databases, or other services and need to access them remotely.

7. Dynamic DNS:

Users with dynamic IP addresses from their internet service providers discover how to set up dynamic DNS (Domain Name System). This allows them to connect to their Raspberry Pi 5 using a hostname rather than an IP address, even when the IP address changes dynamically.

In conclusion, the "Networking and Connectivity" section of the user guide equips users with the knowledge and skills to establish and manage network connections on their Raspberry Pi 5. Whether configuring Wi-Fi or Ethernet, troubleshooting network issues, enabling secure remote access with SSH, or exploring advanced networking features, users gain a comprehensive understanding of networking essentials for their Raspberry Pi projects. This foundational knowledge sets the stage for users to seamlessly integrate their Raspberry Pi 5 into various network environments, enabling diverse applications and functionalities.

CHAPTER EIGHT: Projects and Applications

DIY Projects and Ideas

The Raspberry Pi 5 is not just a single-board computer; it's a versatile platform that invites users to unleash their creativity through a myriad of do-it-yourself (DIY) projects. This section of the user guide sparks inspiration by presenting a variety of projects and ideas, ranging from beginner-friendly endeavors to more advanced applications.

1. Home Automation with Smart Mirror:

Transforming a traditional mirror into a smart mirror is a popular DIY project. Users learn how to integrate a Raspberry Pi 5 with a two-way mirror, displaying useful information like weather, calendar events, and news headlines. This project combines hardware and software elements, providing an engaging introduction to physical computing.

2. Media Center with Kodi or Plex:

Users looking to turn their Raspberry Pi 5 into a media center explore projects using media server applications like Kodi or Plex. The guide covers installing and configuring these applications, enabling users to centralize their media libraries and stream content to various devices.

3. Security Camera System:

Turning the Raspberry Pi 5 into a security camera system is a practical and cost-effective project. Users learn how to set up motion detection, configure cameras, and store footage locally or in the cloud. This project enhances home security and showcases the Raspberry Pi's capabilities in surveillance applications.

4. Weather Station with Sensors:

Weather enthusiasts embark on a DIY weather station project using sensors connected to the Raspberry Pi 5. Users explore interfacing with sensors like temperature and humidity sensors, collecting data, and visualizing it through web-based dashboards. This project provides hands-on experience with hardware integration and data visualization.

5. Gaming Console with RetroPie:

Retro gaming enthusiasts discover how to transform their Raspberry Pi 5 into a retro gaming console using RetroPie. The guide covers installing the RetroPie software, configuring controllers, and loading classic games from various gaming platforms. This project offers a nostalgic gaming experience and showcases the Raspberry Pi's capabilities in emulation.

6. Home Assistant for Smart Home Control:

Creating a smart home control center using Home Assistant is explored in this project. Users integrate the Raspberry Pi 5 with smart devices, enabling centralized control through a user-friendly interface. This project emphasizes home automation and customization possibilities.

7. Personal Web Server:

Users interested in web development set up a personal web server on their Raspberry Pi 5. The guide covers installing web server software like Apache or Nginx, configuring domain names, and hosting websites. This project is an entry point for users exploring web development and hosting.

8. AI and Machine Learning Projects:

Advanced users keen on exploring artificial intelligence (AI) and machine learning (ML) dive into projects that leverage the Raspberry Pi 5's computational capabilities. Examples include image recognition, voice assistants, or even training custom machine learning models using frameworks like TensorFlow Lite.

Installing and Configuring Applications

With the Raspberry Pi 5 serving as a compact computing powerhouse, users can enhance its functionality by installing and configuring various applications. This section of the user guide guides users through the process of expanding the capabilities of their Raspberry Pi 5 by introducing essential applications and providing step-by-step instructions for installation and configuration.

1. Package Management with APT:

Users are introduced to Advanced Package Tool (APT), the package manager for Raspberry Pi OS. The guide covers basic APT commands for installing, updating, and removing software packages. Users gain confidence in managing software installations through the terminal.

2. Web Browsing with Chromium:

The Raspberry Pi 5's enhanced processing power enables a smoother web browsing experience. Users learn how to install the Chromium browser, optimized for the Raspberry Pi, expanding their access to online content directly from their Raspberry Pi 5.

3. Office Suite with LibreOffice:

Productivity is enhanced by installing LibreOffice, a powerful and open-source office suite. Users explore the installation process and learn how to create documents, spreadsheets, and presentations on their Raspberry Pi 5. This application transforms the Raspberry Pi into a productivity tool.

4. Programming Environments:

Tailored for programming enthusiasts, the guide covers installing popular programming environments on the Raspberry Pi 5. Users explore IDEs like Thonny, Visual Studio Code, or lightweight editors like Geany, empowering them to write, test, and debug code efficiently.

5. Multimedia and VLC Media Player:

Users keen on multimedia experiences learn how to install VLC Media Player on their Raspberry Pi 5. This versatile media player supports various audio and video formats, turning the Raspberry Pi into a multimedia center for entertainment.

6. Remote Desktop Applications:

Users exploring remote desktop functionality discover applications like RealVNC or XRDP. The guide covers the installation and configuration of these tools, enabling users to access their Raspberry Pi 5's desktop remotely from other devices.

7. Docker for Containerization:

Advanced users delve into the world of containerization with Docker. The guide introduces Docker on the Raspberry Pi 5, covering installation and basic usage. Users learn how to deploy and manage applications in containers, enhancing flexibility and efficiency.

8. Network Monitoring with Wireshark:

For users interested in network analysis, Wireshark is introduced as a powerful tool.

The guide covers installing Wireshark on the Raspberry Pi 5, providing insights into network traffic and protocols for troubleshooting or educational purposes.

9. Home Automation Applications:

Building on the DIY home automation project, users explore additional home automation applications. This may include platforms like OpenHAB or Node-RED

CHAPTER NINE: Troubleshooting

Common Issues and Solutions

The Raspberry Pi 5, while a powerful and versatile device, may encounter challenges and issues during its usage. This section of the user guide serves as a comprehensive troubleshooting resource, providing insights into common problems users may encounter and offering step-by-step solutions to address these issues effectively.

1. Power-related Issues:

Many Raspberry Pi issues stem from power-related issues. Users are guided through troubleshooting inadequate power supplies, fluctuating power, or issues with USB cables. Understanding the importance of using a reliable power source and proper cables helps prevent various stability and booting problems.

2. SD Card and Storage Problems:

SD card issues can lead to system instability and data corruption. Users learn how to troubleshoot problems such as corrupted file systems, read/write errors, or insufficient storage space. Best practices for selecting high-quality SD cards and periodic backups are emphasized.

3. Boot Problems:

Users encountering boot problems, such as a failure to boot or stuck at the rainbow screen, find solutions in this guide. Troubleshooting steps cover issues with the boot partition, incorrect operating system installations, or corrupted firmware. Users gain insights into resolving these issues and ensuring a smooth boot process.

4. Network Connectivity Challenges:

Troubleshooting network connectivity issues, whether with Wi-Fi or Ethernet, is covered comprehensively. Users learn to diagnose problems related to incorrect credentials, IP address conflicts, or hardware-related issues. Understanding these common networking challenges ensures stable and reliable connections.

5. Display and HDMI Issues:

Users experiencing problems with displays, HDMI connections, or resolution settings find step-by-step solutions in this section. Troubleshooting covers issues such as no display output, incorrect resolution settings, or problems with HDMI cables. Users gain insights into adjusting display configurations for optimal performance.

6. Peripheral Device Compatibility:

Compatibility issues with peripherals like USB devices, keyboards, or mice are addressed in this guide. Users learn how to troubleshoot problems arising from incompatible devices, driver issues, or insufficient power supply to connected peripherals. This section emphasizes the importance of using supported peripherals.

7. Software Update and Upgrade Problems:

Users encountering difficulties with software updates or upgrades receive guidance on troubleshooting these issues. Common problems include failed updates, package conflicts, or issues with repositories. The guide covers solutions for resolving these problems and keeping the Raspberry Pi 5's software up-to-date.

Troubleshooting Hardware and Software Problems

1. Diagnosing Hardware Failures:

This section provides a systematic approach to diagnosing potential hardware failures on the Raspberry Pi 5. Users learn how to identify faulty components, check for physical damage, and use diagnostic tools to assess the health of critical hardware elements. Troubleshooting steps cover components such as the microSD card, power supply, GPIO pins, and USB ports.

2. Temperature and Cooling Issues:

Overheating can impact the Raspberry Pi 5's performance and stability. Users discover how to monitor temperature levels and implement cooling solutions, such as heat sinks or fans, to prevent thermal throttling. Troubleshooting overheating issues ensures optimal performance, especially in resource-intensive applications.

3. Identifying Software Conflicts:

Software conflicts can lead to unexpected behavior or system crashes. Users are guided through methods to identify and resolve software conflicts, including issues with incompatible software packages, conflicting configurations, or dependencies. Troubleshooting software conflicts enhances system stability and performance.

4. Analyzing System Logs:

Understanding system logs is a valuable skill for troubleshooting. Users learn how to analyze system logs to identify error messages, warnings, or patterns indicating potential issues. This section covers accessing logs, interpreting log entries, and using log information to diagnose and resolve problems.

5. Recovering from System Crashes:

In the event of a system crash or unresponsive state, users gain insights into recovery procedures. Troubleshooting steps cover methods for restarting the Raspberry Pi 5, accessing recovery modes, and restoring functionality after a crash. This knowledge ensures users can recover from unexpected system behavior efficiently.

6. Debugging Software Issues:

Debugging techniques are introduced for users encountering software issues or errors in their programs. Users learn how to use debugging tools, interpret error messages, and trace the execution of their code. This section enhances users' ability to identify and fix programming errors effectively.

7. Security and Malware Concerns:

Addressing security and malware concerns is a critical aspect of troubleshooting. Users learn how to detect and mitigate security threats, implement best practices for securing their Raspberry Pi 5, and recognize potential signs of malware or unauthorized access. This section emphasizes proactive measures to enhance the device's security posture.

In conclusion, the "Troubleshooting" section of the user guide equips users with the knowledge and skills needed to address a wide range of issues that may arise during the usage of the Raspberry Pi 5. Whether dealing with common problems related to power, storage, or connectivity, or delving into more complex hardware and software troubleshooting scenarios, users gain the confidence to diagnose, troubleshoot, and resolve issues efficiently. This comprehensive troubleshooting resource empowers users to maintain the stability and reliability of their Raspberry Pi 5, ensuring a smooth and enjoyable computing experience.

CHAPTER TEN: Advanced Topics

Overclocking

Overclocking is an advanced technique that involves pushing the hardware components of the Raspberry Pi 5 beyond their default specifications to achieve enhanced performance. While overclocking can yield noticeable improvements, users should approach it with caution, as it can also lead to increased heat generation and potential stability issues. This section of the user guide explores the intricacies of overclocking on the Raspberry Pi 5, providing users with the knowledge to optimize their device's performance safely.

1. Understanding Overclocking:

Users are introduced to the concept of overclocking, explaining how it involves adjusting the clock speeds of the CPU, GPU, and memory components to achieve higher processing capabilities. The guide outlines the benefits and potential risks associated with overclocking, emphasizing the importance of responsible and gradual adjustments.

2. Raspberry Pi Configuration Tool:

The guide walks users through using the Raspberry Pi Configuration Tool, a user-friendly interface for adjusting overclocking settings. Users gain insights into adjusting parameters such as CPU frequency, GPU frequency, and memory frequency, understanding the impact of each adjustment on system performance.

3. Overclocking Profiles:

Users learn about predefined overclocking profiles that cater to different performance needs. Profiles may include "Modest," "Medium," and "Turbo," with each providing a different level of overclocking.

This section educates users on selecting an appropriate profile based on their usage requirements and understanding the implications of each choice.

4. Monitoring and Stability Testing:

Overclocking involves a delicate balance between performance gains and system stability. Users discover methods for monitoring system temperatures, ensuring that the device doesn't overheat during overclocking. Stability testing tools are introduced, enabling users to stress-test their Raspberry Pi 5 to ensure reliability under increased clock speeds.

5. Heat Dissipation and Cooling Solutions:

Increased clock speeds generate more heat, and users learn about effective cooling solutions to manage temperatures during overclocking. This section covers the use of heat sinks, fans, or even liquid cooling solutions to maintain optimal operating temperatures. Proper cooling is crucial for preventing thermal throttling and ensuring the longevity of the hardware.

Customization and Tweaks

Customization and tweaks allow users to tailor their Raspberry Pi 5 experience to meet specific preferences and requirements. From modifying the appearance of the desktop environment to optimizing system settings, this section of the user guide explores advanced customization options that empower users to create a personalized and efficient computing environment.

1. Desktop Environment Customization:

Users delve into customizing the appearance of their desktop environment. This includes adjusting themes, changing wallpapers, and customizing icons and fonts. The guide introduces tools and commands for modifying the graphical interface to reflect individual preferences.

2. Boot Configurations:

Advanced users explore customizing boot configurations to optimize the startup process. This may involve adjusting the boot order, specifying boot options, or even reducing boot time by disabling unnecessary services. Users gain insights into the boot configuration files and how to modify them safely.

3. Optimizing Power Settings:

Power optimization is crucial for users seeking to maximize energy efficiency or extend battery life in portable Raspberry Pi 5 projects. The guide covers adjusting power settings, including CPU scaling, to balance performance with power consumption. Users learn how to tailor power profiles to suit their specific usage scenarios.

4. File System Tweaks:

Optimizing the file system can enhance read and write performance. Users learn about advanced file system tweaks, such as adjusting file system parameters and optimizing the use of swap space. This section provides guidance on balancing file system optimizations with considerations for data integrity and reliability.

5. Kernel Parameters and Modules:

Users interested in fine-tuning the Linux kernel on their Raspberry Pi 5 explore kernel parameters and modules. The guide covers adjusting kernel parameters to optimize performance and stability. Users gain insights into loading or unloading kernel modules to customize the operating system's functionality.

6. System Resource Management:

Managing system resources effectively is essential for a responsive and efficient computing experience. Users learn about advanced tools and commands for monitoring and managing system resources, including CPU, memory, and disk usage. Techniques such as process prioritization and resource limits are explored.

Security Best Practices

Securing the Raspberry Pi 5 is a critical consideration, especially as users engage in various projects and connect their devices to networks. This section of the user guide delves into security best practices, equipping users with the knowledge and tools to protect their Raspberry Pi 5 from potential threats and unauthorized access.

1. Updating and Patching:

Keeping the operating system and software up-to-date is fundamental for security. Users learn about the importance of regular updates and security patches to address vulnerabilities. The guide covers updating the Raspberry Pi 5 using package managers and staying informed about security advisories.

2. Firewall Configuration:

Configuring a firewall is a crucial step in securing the Raspberry Pi 5 from unauthorized access. Users discover how to set up and configure a firewall, restricting incoming and outgoing network traffic. This section provides guidance on defining rules to allow or deny specific connections.

3. User Account Management:

Users gain insights into effective user account management for enhanced security. The guide covers creating and managing user accounts, setting strong passwords, and understanding user privileges. Users learn about the importance of not using the default "pi" user for increased security.

4. SSH Security:

As SSH is a common method for remote access, securing SSH is paramount. Users explore advanced SSH security practices, including disabling password authentication in favor of key-based authentication. The guide covers generating SSH key pairs, configuring SSH to use keys, and managing authorized_keys. Users also learn how to change the default SSH port for an additional layer of security.

5. Network Segmentation:

Segregating networks is a strategic approach to enhance security. Users learn about network segmentation techniques, such as creating a dedicated network for IoT devices or separating internal and external-facing services. This section provides guidance on configuring network interfaces and implementing VLANs if supported.

6. Intrusion Detection and Prevention:

Implementing intrusion detection and prevention measures is explored in this guide. Users learn about tools and techniques for monitoring network traffic, detecting anomalies, and preventing unauthorized access. The guide introduces applications like Fail2Ban, which automatically blocks IP addresses exhibiting suspicious behavior.

7. Regular Backups:

Data loss can occur due to various reasons, including hardware failures or security incidents. Users discover the importance of regular backups to safeguard critical data. The guide covers backup strategies, tools, and scheduling automated backups to external storage or cloud services.

8. Physical Security Considerations:

Physical security is often overlooked but is a crucial aspect of overall device security. Users learn about physical security considerations, including securing the physical environment, using tamper-resistant cases, and implementing measures to prevent unauthorized access to the Raspberry Pi 5 hardware.

9. Two-Factor Authentication (2FA):

Strengthening access controls with two-factor authentication is covered in this section. Users explore the implementation of 2FA for accessing critical services on the Raspberry Pi 5. The guide introduces tools and methods for integrating 2FA, enhancing authentication security.

10. Monitoring and Auditing:

Effective security involves continuous monitoring and auditing of system activities. Users learn about tools for monitoring logs, tracking user activities, and auditing system changes. This section emphasizes the importance of proactive monitoring to detect and respond to security incidents promptly.

11. Security Awareness and Education:

Users are encouraged to prioritize security awareness and education. The guide emphasizes the significance of staying informed about security best practices, emerging threats, and ongoing vulnerabilities. Users are guided to participate in the Raspberry Pi community, forums, and security discussions to enhance their knowledge.

In conclusion, the "Advanced Topics" section of the user guide provides users with the tools and knowledge to explore advanced aspects of Raspberry Pi 5 usage. Whether seeking to push the device's performance limits through overclocking, customizing the environment for optimal efficiency, or implementing robust security measures, users gain the insights needed to navigate these advanced topics responsibly. By combining performance optimization, customization, and security best practices, users can elevate their Raspberry Pi 5 experience and confidently engage in a diverse range of projects and applications.

Appendix

Technical Specifications

Understanding the technical specifications of the Raspberry Pi 5 is essential for making informed decisions about its usage and capabilities. This section of the user guide provides a comprehensive overview of the Raspberry Pi 5's technical specifications, detailing its hardware components, connectivity options, and performance characteristics.

1. Processor:

The Raspberry Pi 5 is powered by a quad-core ARM Cortex-A76 CPU, offering improved performance compared to its predecessors. Users gain insights into the processor's architecture, clock speed, and capabilities, understanding its role in executing tasks and running applications.

2. Graphics Processing Unit (GPU):

The GPU on the Raspberry Pi 5 is a VideoCore VI, providing enhanced graphics performance. This section outlines the GPU's specifications, including its clock speed, support for graphics APIs, and capabilities for handling multimedia tasks and graphical interfaces.

3. **Memory (RAM):

RAM is crucial for multitasking and overall system performance. Users learn about the Raspberry Pi 5's RAM specifications, including the amount of onboard RAM available for applications and processes. This information guides users in optimizing their usage of system memory.

4. **Storage Options:

The Raspberry Pi 5 supports microSD cards for storage. This section details the compatibility, maximum supported capacity, and considerations for selecting high-performance microSD cards. Users gain insights into optimizing storage for reliability and performance.

5. **Connectivity:

Connectivity is a key aspect of the Raspberry Pi 5's versatility. Users explore the device's USB ports, Ethernet port, and wireless capabilities, including Wi-Fi and Bluetooth. This section provides information on data transfer rates, networking protocols, and compatibility with various peripherals.

6. Video and Audio Output:

Understanding video and audio output options is essential for connecting the Raspberry Pi 5 to displays and audio devices. Users learn about HDMI specifications, audio output options, and supported resolutions. This information aids users in configuring optimal display and audio setups.

7. **GPIO Pins:

The General-Purpose Input/Output (GPIO) pins on the Raspberry Pi 5 facilitate hardware interfacing and project development. This section outlines the GPIO pin layout, pin functions, and the potential for hardware expansion and customization. Users gain a foundational understanding of using GPIO pins for interfacing with sensors, actuators, and other components.

8. Power Requirements:

Power considerations are critical for the stable operation of the Raspberry Pi 5. This section details the device's power requirements, including voltage and current specifications. Users gain insights into selecting suitable power supplies to ensure reliable and efficient performance.

9. Form Factor and Dimensions:

The physical dimensions of the Raspberry Pi 5, including its form factor and size, are outlined in this section. Users gain a sense of the device's footprint, aiding in the selection of enclosures, cases, or integration into various projects with space constraints.

Glossary

The glossary serves as a reference guide, providing definitions and explanations for terms and acronyms commonly encountered in the context of the Raspberry Pi 5 and related technologies. This section aids users in understanding technical jargon, fostering clarity and comprehension throughout their exploration of the Raspberry Pi ecosystem.

1. ARM Architecture:

An acronym for Advanced RISC Machine, ARM is a family of Reduced Instruction Set Computing (RISC) architectures for computer processors. The Raspberry Pi 5 utilizes an ARM-based CPU, emphasizing efficiency and performance in a compact form factor.

2. GPIO (General-Purpose Input/Output):

GPIO refers to pins on the Raspberry Pi that can be configured for input or output. These pins allow the Raspberry Pi to interface with external hardware components, such as sensors, LEDs, and motors, providing flexibility for project development.

3. GPU (Graphics Processing Unit):

The GPU is a specialized processor designed to handle graphical tasks efficiently. In the context of the Raspberry Pi 5, the GPU, known as VideoCore VI, contributes to graphics rendering, multimedia processing, and overall graphical performance.

4. MicroSD Card:

A microSD card is a type of removable flash memory card used for storage in the

Raspberry Pi 5. It serves as the primary storage medium for the operating system, applications, and user data.

5. RAM (Random Access Memory):

RAM is volatile memory used by the Raspberry Pi 5 to store data temporarily during operation. It is essential for running applications and multitasking. The amount of RAM directly influences the device's ability to handle concurrent tasks.

6. HDMI (High-Definition Multimedia Interface):

HDMI is a standard for transmitting high-definition audio and video signals between devices. The Raspberry Pi 5 features an HDMI port for connecting to displays and TVs, supporting various resolutions and multimedia content.

7. Wi-Fi and Bluetooth:

The Raspberry Pi 5 is equipped with wireless connectivity options, including Wi-Fi for network access and Bluetooth for connecting to peripherals such as keyboards, mice, and other devices.

8. Ethernet:

The Ethernet port on the Raspberry Pi 5 allows for a wired network connection. It supports reliable and high-speed data transfer, making it suitable for scenarios where a stable and fast network connection is preferred.

9. Overclocking:

Overclocking involves increasing the clock speeds of the CPU, GPU, or memory components to achieve higher performance. Users may engage in overclocking to push the limits of the Raspberry Pi 5's capabilities, but caution is advised to prevent stability issues.

10. **GPIO Pins:

GPIO pins on the Raspberry Pi are configurable pins that can be set to either input or output. They play a crucial role in interfacing with external hardware components and are often used in electronics and project development.

11. **SSH (Secure Shell):

SSH is a cryptographic network protocol that provides secure communication over an unsecured network. It is commonly used for remote access to the command-line interface of the Raspberry Pi 5, allowing users to control and manage the device.

12. VLAN (Virtual Local Area Network):

VLANs are used for network segmentation, allowing users to create isolated networks within a larger network infrastructure. This can enhance security and optimize network performance in specific use cases.

13. 2FA (Two-Factor Authentication):

2FA adds an additional layer of security beyond traditional username and password authentication. Users typically need to provide a second form of verification, such as a code from a mobile app or a hardware token, to access secured services.

This glossary aims to demystify technical terms and acronyms, enabling users to navigate the Raspberry Pi 5 ecosystem with confidence and clarity. As users refer to the glossary, they can deepen their understanding of the technical landscape and make informed decisions in their Raspberry Pi 5 endeavors.

www.ingramcontent.com/pod-product-compliance
Lightning Source LLC
LaVergne TN
LVHW051715050326
832903LV00032B/4209

* 9 7 9 8 8 7 7 3 8 7 5 4 6 *